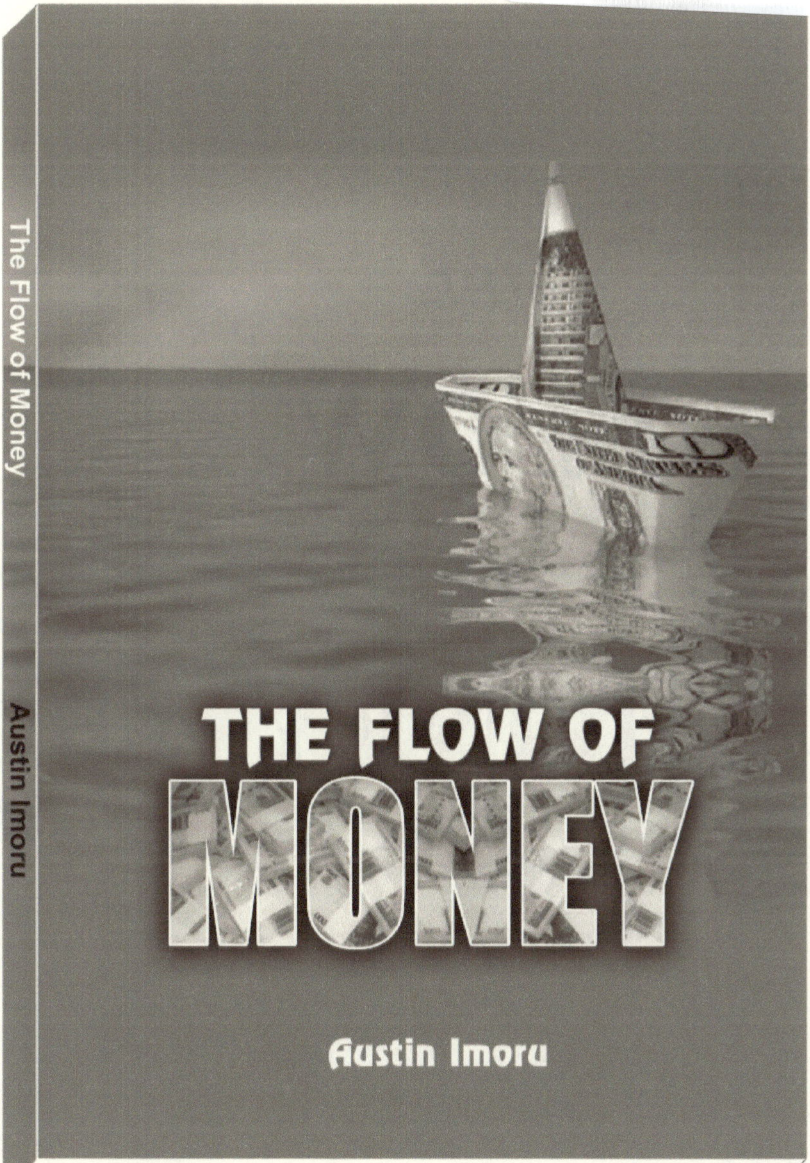
The Flow of Money
Austin Imoru
THE FLOW OF
MONEY
Austin Imoru

THE
FLOW
OF
MONEY

How Today's Billionaires are Made

THE FLOW OF MONEY

First published in 2016
By FineLines Publishers
www.finelinespublishers.com
ISBN: 9781079668117

for FineLines Publishers

All rights reserved. No part of this Publication may be reproduced, stored in retrieval system, or transmitted in any form or by any means, electronic, mechanical, photocopying, recording, or otherwise without the prior permission of the Publisher.

© 2019 By Austin Imoru

Contents

1. Introduction
2. Inventing Money
3. Where Do Money Flow?
4. Making Money Flow towards You
5. They Made it Easy
6. Opportunity Calls
7. Take Action Now

Introduction

Inventing money has never been easier. This is the post 21st Century, the most interesting times to be alive. It is an era where new billionaires keep showing up. The likes of Mark Zackeberg of Facebook are springing up of several industries. According to Bloomberg recent reports, an average of 1,700 becomes first time millionaires every day in America. Even in Africa many young people, the likes of Linda Ikeji are springing up, out from nowhere to become millionaires.

All these are made possible because many are getting to know the secret of inventing their money. You too can learn this secret and start inventing your own money. It is now a cliché that every digit out there called money was invented either by corporate institute like banks and countries or by certain individuals.

This book will teach you to master the secret of inventing money. Hard or smart work wouldn't help you to become really wealthy, if you don't know the secret that will unlock the spin that leads to the direction that money flows. It works anywhere in the world. It has helped many to invent their billions. It is your turn to learn the secret.

Read, learn and activate the most powerful secret that has led many to a world of unlimited wealth. It will help you predict any market or business and make all your hard or smart work count. See you on the other side where money flows.

Austin Imoru

Flow One

Inventing Money

I can count more than 12 wealthy men that I know, who seems not to be working at any particular office at the moment but are still quite wealthy. When asked, they simply say, they are business people. Of recent, I ran into another young lady, married with one child. She was very much financially comfortable, she has so much going on for her and she also said, she was a business person.

"What exactly do you do madam?" I asked. "Why," she replied, "I run the most powerful business in the world from anywhere I might be, with my smartphone or laptop."

I was dump-founded, but like most young men in search of greatness, I was far from satisfied with that kind of reply. She has to cough it all out, letter by letter, step by step, how this so called 'most powerful business' works. I was determined to know what she knows. She was too relaxed and way too pretty to be a hustler.

You see, this wasn't my first encounter with young wealthy fellows like her. Few months ago, I ran into a young man. Just by looking at him, one could tell that this young man was living in great affluent in a society of so much lack. His well-trimmed moustache perfectly resting upon his immaculate royal skin spoke of nothing but a good life. A pastor friend and I came to visit him, to pray for his wife who just put to bed.

When we entered his living room, I was instantly blown away by the out of this world furniture and the unbelievable electronic gadgets that garnished the spacious apartment. I couldn't help but noticed that all the gadgets in the apartment were manipulated by a single remote control. I mean all the gadgets, including the window blinds, the weird looking ceiling fans, air conditioners, home theatre and so on.

I could barely wait for the pastor to finish his prayers before I fired my first question at Mr. Flexible, as the house owner was fondly called. "What exactly do you do sir?" I asked.

He looked at me, hard and long, before saying, "I am a businessman."

"What kind of business sir," I fired back, "if you don't mind me asking?"

My pastor friend was very uncomfortable with my line of questions. He cuts in very quickly and announced that we will be leaving. I wasn't satisfied yet, so I insist that Mr. Flexible should please educate me on how to run successful businesses as the pastor is not a businessman. He hesitated a little before adding that he does his own business.

Still not satisfied, I asked, "how can someone like me get to know how to run a viable business like yours?" You wouldn't blame me, I was curious. He was married to a Regional Bank Manager, and he a seemly lay-about, who doesn't go to work every day, and without any known business brand name, was by far richer than the wife. I wanted to know all that made him Mr. Flexible.

Well, he never really answered my questions; he only threw a few questions and statements at me. First, he asked, "do you have the statistic of where money is really going in this country? I had no idea what he was talking about. Where is money going? I repeatedly asked myself? Is that how he got all this wealth?

Secondly, he asked, "how would you feel, if you don't have to pay tax but earn heavily and the government will even compensate you from time to time, with favourable policies. "

"That would be fantastic," I said, "but does such a thing exist?"

Mr. Flexible looked hard at me, as if wondering where I came from. "Of course, you wouldn't need to face the embarrassing Government taxes. Such businesses do exist, my friend," he stressed with so much finality that dissolve all my doubts. Though I couldn't fully comprehend what he was saying, yet I was convince that he knew something I didn't know. Some secret on how things work around here.

As I was still pondering upon his insinuations, he said, "those who think that everyone that is wealthy must be a contractor with Oil Companies or a top management staff of one multinational or at the very least, a fraudulent person, don't know the secret behind real flow of wealth."

"What do you mean?" I stammered what sounded more like a disagreement than a question.

"Well," he postulated slowly, "don't take my word for it, start by acquiring the statistics of where money flows in this country and you wouldn't have to work another day of your life."

I couldn't dig deeper to know more, he immediately waved us goodbye and disappeared behind his artistically flushed designer living room door. I wanted to hear more, but my pastor friend wouldn't let me. He was too much in a hurry to learn the simple truth about quantum progress in life.

Without any double in me, I knew Mr. Flexible was right; there are three kinds of people out there;

> 1.) Those who think that everyone that is wealthy must be a contractor with Oil Companies, a banker or a top

management staff of a big multi-national firm.

2.) Those who think that everyone that is wealthy must be fraudulent and

3.) Those who think that real wealth is hidden in principles or what some call the secret of the flow of money which varies from place to place.

It was after my first encounter with Mr. Flexible that I made it a duty to make sure I interview any wealthy person I ever encountered. I have since interviewed more than forty wealthy young people. The interesting thing about those who are truly financially comfortable, is that they were all business people, who does their business strategically and invest almost perfectly in a consistent level on what the ordinary person will never consider investing on.

One common trait with all of them is the strong believe that real wealth is hidden in principles or the secret of the flow of money, which gives you the courage to see opportunities in hidden places and become the first to invest. I also realised that all wealthy people in our country are persistently after the statistics of where money flows. Many of them said, it is the reason they open the newspaper every morning. While other people are looking at political stories and celebrity gossips, these men are drawing the lines and seeking for the flow of money.

Without any doubt, this seems to me as the major distinction between the very wealthy and the average people.

Flow two

Where Do Money Flow?

Someone strongly posited that you can tell a man's future by what he look at daily in the Newspapers or Tabloids. I totally agree. I have often said, that those who see nothing in the daily papers but gossips are liable to die in self-pity. Those who see opportunity in every line are destined to stain the annals of greatness with the ink of their exploits.

If you really want to find the flow of money, start by asking yourself, what people are spending money on. In a country like Nigeria majority of the people erroneously think that a larger percentage of the country's wealth is found in the country's Oil wells. However, they are often stranded when they can't figure out how they can secure a part of the wealth of the Oil Wells for themselves. What they don't know is that though most people use oil as fuel, kerosene or diesel; majority of the people use water more than they use fuel, kerosene or diesel put together.

Your money is in people. Whether your trade is water or oil, you must sell to people. Therefore, your share of the collective wealth is determined by what the people are willing to spend their money on. They would spend their money on fuel, kerosene or diesel and consider it as luxury, while drinking water is a necessary call of nature. They would rather spend on water to stay alive than spend on oil.

You will find gold in people, when you take time to know what they spend their money on, that is the flow of money. When you strategically wait for them where they are going to spend their money because of necessity you will always have enough money.

Beside water there are some basic necessities now that are like breathing air in our society. Most people can't do without them. Some are like basic necessities that many believe will bring them more money. So they will be willing to purchase it even with their last cent. If you think deeply you will find such necessities. They are gold mines to wealth; the flow of money is the key.

Let's see people are spending money on, in any given country, using Nigeria as a case-study. Here is a huge example that will shock you about how Nigerians spend their money and on what;

- Nigerians spend 149.1 billion naira on House rent monthly
- Nigerians spend 128 billion naira on Petrol monthly
- Nigerians spend 144.8 billion naira on Kerosene monthly

- Nigerians spend 91.8 billion naira on electricity monthly

- Nigerians spend N447.8 billion naira on recharge cards monthly

The above spending stats are culled from the statistics of an ICT expert, Mr. Gbenga Oyebode of Aluko & Oyebode law firm (Vanguard, March 19, 2014)

From the above chart, where is money going to in the Nigerian situation? What are Nigerians spending their money on? I tell you friend, this is the big secret that makes it possible for some folks to become billionaires from the comfort of their homes. It allows them to predict the market and the best place and time to invest their money.

With just a business name, with no formal office place, I have seen many young Nigerians make millions just by understanding the flow of money. Like Mr. Flexible from our earlier story, you too can be all that you can dare dream if you would understand the flow of money.

The above statistic is just one of the many researches we can embark on to measure how and where money flows and make strategic plan to cut out a percentage for ourselves. If for example, I want to go into the Recharge Card business, which happens to be the highest spending flow of money for Nigerians, I must determine what percentage of the 447.8 billion naira monthly that I want. I can then go ahead to strategize on how to secure that percentage.

Knowing where money flows is to know what people around you spend money on the most. You can always determine this by looking at the general statistics from corporate bodies, Central Bank, per share capital of a host of companies in specific industries and what you and your neighbours are spending your money on.

Understanding the flow of money will never allow you to overlook any scarce commodity again in your life. When a certain commodity is scarce in the market and you like several others are in need of it. Those who understand the flow of money, will investigate why. If it is because of high demand, they see money flowing in a direction that is in urgent need of strategic investment.

Another factor that can help you determine the flow of money could be found when we keenly consider the shifting cultural spending and the basic human needs that necessitate spending. Talking about the shifting culture, you need to know the present or in-coming trend that people can easily get attached to. The basic human needs are food, water, shelter, comfort and so on. People will always spend to meet their basic needs and at the same time spend to meet shifting cultural necessities.

Now, whether it is cultural necessities or basic needs, the factors that make the difference is the frequency and velocity of the demand. Knowing the flow will help you strategize better to partake in the flow.

To effectively take advantage of this secret, you must realize that there is always a flow. Money is currency because it flows in current. The reason some people lack money is because it is not flowing in their direction. Money will always come to those who understand its flow and how to harness the flow.

Acquiring great wealth is never a function of chance, if by chance you stumble upon money; chances are you will not keep it for long. This is because, it will flow to the man who understands the direction of it flow and has built up strategies to harvest it.

Those who stumble upon money by chance, always loose it by chance. Money flows in certain directions that knowing the secret will help you predict every time. Every wealthy person I have ever interviewed has mastered how to make money flow towards them.

This is the answer to the million dollar question many people have been asking for so many years now. "Why is it that the rich are getting richer?" It is pretty simple, there is no conspiracy anywhere. The rich know something the poor don't know. A secret that help them predict the flow of money consistently.

While the poor rely on chance and hard work, the rich are busy spending their time and money searching for the flow of money. This works for them every time and they are able to teach it to their children. Hard work alone can't produce great wealth; great wealth comes through definite truth of knowing how and where money flows.

This truth is not only for the rich, it is for everyone. Now you have found the secret, the truth behind great wealth. You can take advantage of this simple but profound truth and create your own reality of tremendous wealth. Life answers to principles; make this one count. Remember, it works anywhere, any time and for anyone who put it to work. Get working.

Flow three

Making Money Flow towards You

This is a deliberate, as well as strategic business, it doesn't happen by chance. Knowing the spending flow (flow of money) is one thing; getting the flow to come to you is another. Many people will see the Oyebode's statistics we presented above and decide to go after the Recharge Card Business. They might choose to start big as major dealers, signing up with all the network providers or become a street vendor.

As smart is that may sound, they will end up like anyone else already in the business. They wouldn't make meaningful profit that way. There is a better way, other than joining the traditional flow. There is a way to make the money in the business flow towards you.

I want you to see, the flow of money as the flow of a normal Stream (River). If you know anything about Rivers at all, you would realize that determining the direction where which the current flows is the easy part. You will also realize that joining the current means your direction will be determined by the current and not you. At best you can determine your speed by using a paddle.

Now, think of a fishing festival where a large group of people are flowing with the current of the River while they fish. This is like our traditional business world, everyone doing the same thing. It is always highly competitive and yield very minimal profit or what I called shared profits.

If maximum profit is what you are after, you must not follow the traditional or popular business model. In other words, after understanding the flow of money, you must not jump into the stream and expect to grab a huge percentage of the market's profits.

From Oyebode's statistics, the Recharge Card Business has a monthly spending of 447.8 billion naira, how can you grab at least 2 percent of that spending? The smart thing to do is to go up stream and wait for the current to flow your way. You can make the current flow towards you, or determine how and where it is flowing and strategically position yourself where it will meet you.

The smartest thing to do is to plan how to make the big players of your targeted industry come to you even if it were to be for something as minimal as software. Now if you can make over 9 million Nigerians that use airtime come to you or 25 huge firms that service them, you will have huge profits.

Still sighting the Recharge Card business, since you can't follow the flow of current business trends of becoming a dealer, distributor or street vendor, you must figure out how to make those already in the business come to you for help or support. This is what most post 21st Century emerging billionaires have done in different industries.

How? Consider this. If the new trend in world economy today is Mobile Money, it means that over 89 percent of products will become virtual products, including printing of recharge cards. So, what better ways can you wait for such future? Go virtual of course, start trading on VTU or design a software that will help do the transaction or create an application that synchronizes a particular bank account to a phone, which will automatically credit that phone when transaction are done.

Go virtual before the trend get there. In this case, your up-stream is the virtual world and by all means the current of Recharge Card Business will get to you. Like Mr. Flexible, you amass great riches from the comfort of your room.

Flow four

They Made it Easy

It is genius that makes everyone feels like they can do anything. A genius on the piano makes you feel it is easy and you can do it too. It is simply because they do it with so much ease that gives you the impetus to want to try it out. However money making in the post 21st Century is no stroke of genius at all. It is the actualization and applications of secrets.

Making money has never been easier. Just about anyone armed with the secret of the flow of money and the willingness to engage the truth shared in this material can become millionaire too. Please don't just read this book, I challenge you to act on it and you will be shock how easy it is to become a millionaire in these days and times.

Countless seemly insignificant youth in Africa have acted on this same truth and their achievements were phenomena. They become tremendously wealthy.

Verone Mankou is a Congolese who created a multimillion dollar company called Tech Entrepreneur, he is a man that invents money by simply putting this secret to work. What about Joel Mwale, a Kenyan who built a great company named Skydrop

Enterprises, his ability to invent money is unquestionable. Talking about fast growing Nigerians, the likes of Linda Ikeji of lindaikejiblog and Oluwaseun Osewa founder of Nairaland both invent money in most unconventional ways.

The list is vast and everyone of them saw the flow of great wealth ahead of them and invented a bridge to reach it. Now they are young wealthy people. They didn't cheat to gain great wealth, not employed in multinationals. They invented their money by trading on the secret they found. Now I am sharing that secret with you.

It is a whole new world out there, if you live in this generation and can't invent money, you will have yourself to blame.

Almost every wealthy young person of today, even in Africa emerged from zero financial background to serious wealth. The Nigerian Linda & Oluwaseun plus several others are not left out. The crazy truth about their lifestyle is that it is pretty normal, they can even run their businesses from anywhere in the world, while on vacation, family outing or government functions.

Statistics stated that over half of all U.S. businesses are now based in their owner's home, according to the U.S. Census Bureau. It is no surprise for me at all, because every important business in history started in someone's backyard or garage. It is pretty simple now, arm yourself with the truth shared in this book and get to work.

This material is not intended to share stories but principles that make the stories. I would have share stories with you about young Africans who are topping the world's millionaires chart. They all have very common ideas but with the right information of where to launch their ideas – the direction of the flow of money. The secret they know took them to the upstream of their chosen industries where they strategically waited for the incoming tide.

It is the principle of the flow of money that made all of them. It is the common thing with which all millionaires today are measured. You want to be a millionaire, get to know this principle, practice it and wait upstream for the tides that will bring your millions and billions to you. It works all the time; it has made millionaires and billionaires and will yet make more.

We live in a generation where we can create products and wait for the world to get educated or informed enough to know they need our products more than the food they eat. It has been the prototype that launched most businesses today. It is the principle of the upstream.

Facebook came with a product, social connect that the people were not even aware they needed. The world caught up with it and there goes the money. In Africa, mobile phone came that the people didn't know they needed, yet it bust the market. What about mobile money, who could have thought that farmers and street traders in

Kenya will pay for goods and services with their mobile phones.

Do I need say more? Gossip used to be offensive, but since Oprah made a career out of it, it has since become part of social connect. Linda Ikeji redesigned it in form of a blog, and that simple remix has made her a millionaire. What is your product or services, create the roadmap to the flow of money, climb upstream and strategically wait.

You don't need anyone's permission to be a millionaire today. The permission you need is your understanding of the right principles and the audacity to act on what you know.

I believe those who will lack in the next century are those who refused to act on what they know. Hesitation will be the cross upon which many promising destinies will be hanged. Information will not be the problem, in the coming age; it is already available everywhere.

Flow five

Opportunity Calls

We are never left without opportunities, they are everywhere around us. Of a truth opportunity is the bringer of great wealth. Work becomes hard work without opportunities. Life is punctuated with opportunities for those who pay attention to little details. Those who refuse to go to sleep with the old proverb, which states that 'opportunity comes but once,' often find more opportunities than they can maximize.

The difference between those who maximize the flow of money and those who didn't is in how they see their worlds. For a long while I thought working hard was the secret to great wealth. I also thought opportunities are for those who know how to work smart, with all the right information at their command.

It didn't occur to me until recently that opportunity come to everyone but only those who pay attention to little details get to see and maximize them. There are no special skills needed to have opportunities come to you other than paying attention to details. If you can only raise your observation antenna, you will see that opportunities are all around you.

A wealthy young man once told me that if I were poor it was my fault. I couldn't believe he was saying that. My first thought was that of pride. I thought he was mocking me and out of cruel pomposity, he wanted me to know he was a self-made man.

Then he added that making money is fifty percent 'paying attention' and fifty percent daring; no hard work is required. I thought he must be crazy to think anyone could be rich without hard work.

Who should know better, the man who has been working hard all his life and still has not found real wealth or the man who has been able to build an empire that could compete with most multinationals before he was in his middle forties? I think he should know better.

"Attention and daring are for champions." He said, "you want opportunities to come to you? You must learn to pay attention and you must be daring if you must take advantage of your opportunities."

I have since discovered for myself that there are opportunities everywhere. If you can see all the angles, you will surely find one or two opportunities. In a single business there might be more than twenty dimensions where investment can yield tremendously. You must be able to access several dimensions so you could make informed choice.

Let's look at the Recharge Card Business for instance. At first it might seems as if the only viable dimension to this business is selling recharge cards. While that remains the most visible it is by no means the most viable, there are others when you look closely.

You could look at the card printing angle or distribution angle; maybe VTU angle or bulk sales angle. You could also consider other angles like servicing corporate bodies, families, house wives, government workers, night workers, onshore and offshore workers, doctors, security personnel etc. You could also consider those who convert credits to bundle for easy Internet access.

Angles to this business are numerous to mention. As it is with Recharge Card business so it is with every other business. Make sure you are not just considering the product side of the business, consider the services side as well. As a matter of fact, there are most of the times more opportunities in the service angle than the product angle.

What is your business and from what angle are you cutting out your wealth? Are you aware of the advantages of those other angles and the one you chose? If you most dominate your chosen business category, you must be aware of almost all the angles. You must identify the one most viable, with most opportunities and elasticity to achieve more. You must be aware of the likely future opportunities.

In Kenya, some folks in communication business saw most of the angles that exist and were thus inspired to think of what is possible. Great thinkers are known to be aware of most angles before they invent what could be added. You cannot predict the future of your business if you cannot see most of the business angles.

Those folks in Kenya ended up with one of the most resourceful Mobile Money establishment that exist today. They search most angles in communication and by so doing stumbled upon an unbeatable idea. You too can birth that money minting idea if you can pay attention to opportunities from all angles.

Mobile Money seems to be a new business today. It seems like it is the business of the future. In kenya, M-PESA runs transaction worth over $20,489,472 (N3.3 billion) daily. This is happening in Africa. Imagine the opportunities in this business. Imagine all the angles and what opportunities will shot out when you run this business in much larger countries in the West or in Nigeria.

Can you see the angles; services, products are endless possibilities? You must see the angles if you must see the opportunities. What do you see?

The post 21st Century business will be championed by those who can see opportunities where others see impossibilities. What do you see? Take another look at your business. A closer look, a critical evaluation of all the angles and consider all available opportunities and it will shock you that you have been sitting on a gold mine. What do you see?

Consider the printing business and where it is heading. Now that the world is shrinking into mobile and digital devices, it is time for great and fast thinkers to take advantage of the e-book business. What do you see? See the multiple advantages and seize the opportunities.

What about the New World of Apps? What do you see? He that sees first, will act first. If armed with multiple chances of seeing all the angles, he will win. Business and wealth wouldn't wait for anyone, it flows at the speed of thought. What do you see?

There are over 180 million Nigerians. What opportunities can you see in this huge population; many angles of opportunities or many horns of challenges? The choice is yours; join those that cry or those who see opportunities in every dark cloud. This is your opportunity call. Answer this call and wealth will answer to you. Think opportunity and money will flow towards you.

No matter how bad it may look if you can see the angles, you will find the opportunities.

Flow Six

Take Action Now

In real achievement, action is non-negotiable. You can't bank information and expect to make maximum profit out of it. Banked information will never add money to your bank account. You must act upon the right information to have the desired result. Even professors that love to shelf information still have to share them before he can get paid.

If you have read the principle of the flow of money you need to go upstream right away and harness the power of the flow. You must not wait, take action now. If you don't know where to start, engage the following steps;

1.) Find your rhythm: begin by seeking out the industry where you belong. Personally, I think anyone can fit into any industry, just make sure you pick an enjoyable side of such industry. By enjoyable side, I mean what you enjoy doing. If I picked the information industry for example, there are endless sides to it.

All I need do is to find the side that suits me best.

I can choose to sell information, major on news, sell information aids, trade information access, link people with information, trade countries secrets, repackage information etc. Whichever side or angle you pick, run an access to see whether money flows that way first. You can link whatever industry you are in with anything else.

2.) Find your share in percentage: once you have identify the flow of money in that industry, you then have to pick the percentage of the total flow you want. Build your strategy around the percentage that you want. The bigger the percentage, the more massive action plans you will need to reach your desired goal.

You must realize that whatever industry you find yourself, a certain percentage of the total income of that industry is yours. Until you start to think that way and use actual statistics to build a plan for yourself, you cannot lay claim to that industry. When you make yourself believe that such industry own you a certain percentage, then you will be committed to give it all it takes.

Owning the industry, calling it yours is the secret to achieving big in that industry. You think better when you think the industry depends on you. You become a major player in an industry by thinking from the start that you own a certain percentage.

Think like a billionaire and you would become a billionaire.

3.) Question the existing standards: if you must make a difference in any industry, you must understand how they play in that industry. You cannot expect to dominate an industry you don't know much about. Someone once posited that 'you must know all the laws because there are some you must break.

What limit others in the industry before you came must be the laws, rules or standard by which they play. So, first understand the standards and then, deliberately question them. I assure you, when you do, you will definitely find the way forward. Refuse to be satisfied with the norms and standards of the industry, deliberately seek a better way. Seek like a millionaire, where others wouldn't dare to seek and you will found great treasures.

4.) Prepare and take advantage of the up-stream: now that you know the industry and where its money flows, you must draw a map for the upstream. Seeing into the future of any industry makes you the leader of that industry in no time. What Bill Gate saw in the future of software, made him the leader today.

The Nigeria top female billionaire saw something in Oil-wells that others couldn't see at the time. She took advantage of it and years later, she turn out to be the richest black woman in the world. If you must go far in your industry, you must think of the changes that will occur and the challenges that will show up in the future.

If you have a plan on how to solve a challenge that will likely bedeviled your industry in the future, I guarantee you will lead that industry when the time comes. Load your guns, wait where the antelopes are sure to taxi through and your profits will be unquestionable.

5.) Learn to negotiate: if you are really going to wait upstream, you must learn to negotiate. If you are not aware of anything about negotiation, you must understand my first and second laws of negotiation;

Law #1.) Don't make a deal when you are broke and seriously in need.

Law #2.) Don't break a deal that is urgent. Never let anyone hurry you into concluding a deal when you are not ready.

Are you ready for the new world? How prepare are you for the upstream experience? What you should be doing is getting ready to take advantage of the future. Contrary to what is known by many; the future doesn't wait on men, smart men prepare and wait for the future.

Those who can see the future before it's publicly revealed are rewarded by the public. What are you waiting for, the future or some miracles? If you are waiting for miracles, I would like you to know that miracles are for those who crafted path for their opportunities.

You are the opportunity others are waiting for, the next millionaire or billionaire that will spring up from nowhere if you engage the secrets of the flow of money. Take action now; let massive wealth sail towards your upstream. Take action today!

About the Author

Austin Imoru is a certified dream coach, determined to help others process their dreams into successful realities in any career or fit. He is certified by John C. Maxwell Leadership Training as trainer/coach and Dr. Joshua Freedman of Six-Seconds as Emotional Intelligence (EQ) coach. He believes idleness is a crime to humanity, and believes that anybody can live better if he finds a dream and set sail towards it.

Presently, Austin is working with Start-Ups in Africa with a goal of helping them tell and spread their unique story. His focus is 10 thousand Start-Ups in Africa. To tell your unique start-up story or if you happen to know anyone who needs this, share the web address below with them. You can sign up today, just visit www.startupmarketing.com.ng.

For more about Austin Imoru, visit: www.austinimoru.com

www.ingramcontent.com/pod-product-compliance
Lightning Source LLC
Chambersburg PA
CBHW030018190526
45157CB00016B/3120